NEVER
Forget

Jack Hayford

Anne Graham Lotz

Max Lucado

Henri Nouwen

Charles Stanley

Charles R. Swindoll

W PUBLISHING GROUP™

www.wpublishinggroup.com

A Division of Thomas Nelson, Inc.
www.ThomasNelson.com

Published by W Publishing Group, a Division of Thomas Nelson, Inc., P.O. Box 141000, Nashville, Tennessee 37214.

Compiled and edited by Elizabeth Kea.

Unless otherwise noted, all Scripture quotations are from *The Holy Bible, New Century Version* (NCV), copyright 1987, 1988, 1991 by W Publishing Group, Nashville, TN 37214.

Scripture quotations marked (NIV) are taken from the Holy Bible, New International Version®. NIV®. Copyright © 1973, 1978, 1984 by International Bible Society. Used by permission of Zondervan Publishing House. All rights reserved. Scripture quotations marked (MSG) are from The Message. Copyright © by Eugene H. Peterson 1993, 1994, 1995. Used by permission of NavPress Publishing Group. Scripture quotations marked (NASB) are from the New American Standard Bible®. © Copyright The Lockman Foundation 1960, 1962, 1963, 1968, 1971, 1972, 1973, 1975, 1977. Used by permission. (www.Lockman.org). Scripture quotations marked (TLB) are taken from The Living Bible copyright © 1971. Used by permission of Tyndale House Publishers, Inc., Wheaton, Illinois 60189. All rights reserved. Scripture quotations marked (NKJV) are taken from the New King James Version of the Bible. Copyright © 1979, 1980, 1982, Thomas Nelson, Inc. Publishers. Scripture quotations marked (NRSV) are taken from The New Revised Standard Version of the Bible © 1989 by the Division of Christian Education of the National Council of Churches of Christ in the USA.

Library of Congress Cataloging-in-Publication Data available

ISBN 0-8499-4408-2

Printed in the United States of America
02 03 04 05 06 PHX 5 4 3 2 1

Contents

A Note from the Publisher

September 11, 2001, is a day America and the world will never forget. So many lives were lost: fathers, mothers, sons, daughters, friends, companions. Families from around the world bear the scars of what happened that day. And while the devastation from the attacks of September 11 is unforgettable, many of us find ourselves thrust into the midst of smaller but no less devastating personal catastrophes, and we wonder how we'll cope.

The good news—even *great* news—is that there is hope to be discovered amidst the rubble of tragedy. In this little book, you will find that hope. Through selected writings from leading Christian authors you will find answers to the hard questions of suffering, and you will discover that, in the end, hope prevails.

Preface

Address to the Nation
SEPTEMBER 11, 2001

Today, our fellow citizens, our way of life, our very freedom came under attack in a series of deliberate and deadly terrorist acts. The victims were in airplanes, or in their offices; secretaries, businessmen and women, military and federal workers; moms and dads, friends and neighbors. Thousands of lives were suddenly ended by evil, despicable acts of terror.

The pictures of airplanes flying into buildings, fires burning, huge structures collapsing, have filled us with disbelief, terrible sadness, and a quiet, unyielding anger. These acts of mass murder were intended to frighten our nation into chaos and retreat. But they have failed; our country is strong.

A great people has been moved to defend a great nation. Terrorist attacks can shake the foundations of our biggest buildings, but they cannot touch the foundation of America. These acts shattered steel, but they cannot dent the steel of American resolve.

America was targeted for attack because we're the brightest beacon for freedom and opportunity in the world. And no one will keep that light from shining.

Today, our nation saw evil, the very worst of human nature. And we responded with the best of America—with the daring of our rescue workers, with the caring for strangers and neighbors who came to give blood and help in any way they could. . . .

America and our friends and allies join with all those who want peace and security in the world, and we stand together to win the war against terrorism. Tonight, I ask for your prayers for all those who grieve, for the children whose worlds have been shattered, for all whose sense of safety and security has been threatened. And I pray they will be comforted by a power greater than any of us, spoken through the ages in Psalm 23: "Even though I walk through the valley of the shadow of death, I fear no evil, for You are with me."

This is a day when all Americans from every walk of life unite in our resolve for justice and peace. America has stood down enemies before, and we will do so this time. None of us will ever forget this day. Yet, we go forward to defend freedom and all that is good and just in our world.

—PRESIDENT GEORGE W. BUSH

Where Is God?

Never Forget . . . God Is Near

❖ ❖ ❖

Where Is God?

Many people today are wondering how God could allow the tragedy of September 11, 2001. What could he be thinking? Is God really in control? Can we trust him to run the universe if he would allow terrorists to take the lives of so many people?

It is important to recognize that God dwells in a different realm. He occupies another dimension. "My thoughts are not like your thoughts. Your ways are not like my ways. Just as the heavens are higher than the earth, so are my ways higher than your ways and my thoughts higher than your thoughts" (Isaiah 55:8–9).

Make special note of the word *like*. God's thoughts are not our thoughts, nor are they even *like* ours. We aren't even in the same neighborhood. We're thinking, Preserve the body; he's thinking, Save the soul. We dream of a pay raise. He dreams of raising the dead. We avoid pain and seek peace. God uses pain to bring peace. "I'm going to live before I die," we resolve. "Die so you can live," he instructs. We love what rusts. He loves what endures. We rejoice at our successes. He rejoices at our confessions. We show our children the Nike star with the million-dollar smile and say, "Be like Mike." God points to the crucified carpenter with bloody lips and a torn side and says, "Be like Christ."

Our thoughts are not like God's thoughts. Our ways are not like his ways. He has a different agenda. He dwells in a different dimension. He lives on another plane.

> The heavens tell the glory of God,
>   and the skies announce what
>   his hands have made.
> Day after day they tell the story;
>   night after night they tell it again.
> They have no speech or words;
>   they have no voice to be heard.
> But their message goes out through
>   all the world;
>   their words go everywhere on earth.
>
> (PSALM 19:1–4)

Nature is God's workshop. The sky is his résumé. The universe is his calling card. You want to know who God is? See what he has done. You want to know his power? Take a look at his creation. Curious about his strength? Pay a visit to his home address: 1 Billion Starry Sky Avenue. Want to know his size? Step out into the night and stare at star-light emitted one million years ago. . . .

He is untainted by the atmosphere of sin, unbridled by the time line of history, unhindered by the weariness of the body.

What controls you doesn't control him. What troubles you doesn't trouble him. What fatigues you doesn't fatigue him. Is an eagle disturbed by traffic? No, he rises above it. Is the whale perturbed by a hurricane? Of course not; he plunges beneath it. Is the lion flustered by the mouse standing directly in his way? No, he steps over it.

How much more is God able to soar above, plunge beneath, and step over the troubles of the earth! "What is impossible with man is possible with God" (see Matthew 19:26). Our questions betray our lack of understanding:

How can God be everywhere at one time? (Who says God is bound by a body?)

How can God hear all the prayers that come to him? (Perhaps his ears are different from yours.)

How can God be the Father, the Son, and the

Holy Spirit? (Could it be that heaven has a different set of physics than earth?)

If people down here won't forgive me, how much more am I guilty before a holy God? (Oh, just the opposite. God is always able to give grace when we humans can't—he invented it.)

How vital that we pray, armed with the knowledge that God is in heaven. Pray with any lesser conviction, and our prayers are timid, shallow, and hollow. Look up and see what God has done, and watch how your prayers are energized.

This knowledge gives us confidence as we face the uncertain future. We know that he is in control of the universe, and so we can rest secure. But important also is the knowledge that this God in heaven has chosen to bend near toward earth to see our sorrow and hear our prayers. He is not so far above us that he is not touched by our tears.

Though we may not be able to see his purpose or his plan, the Lord of heaven is on his throne and in firm control of the universe and our lives. So we entrust him with our future. We entrust him with our very lives.

—MAX LUCADO
America Looks Up

❖ ❖ ❖

Aim Your Hard Questions
at God, Not Man

"My God, My God, why have You forsaken Me?"
(Matthew 27:46). . . . It is perhaps the most dra-
matic word spoken from Calvary. It trembles with
emotional anguish, and nothing dramatizes it
more passionately than the heart-piercing cry of
God's Son, feeling a sense of abandonment at the
darkest moment of this very bad day: "Why? Why?
Why have You left Me now?" . . .

This is the central moment of Calvary: it is the
fourth of seven words. It is filled with questions,
with darkness, with a sense of ultimate forsaken-
ness—God forsaken! Even if we never experience
the dimension of Jesus' depression, all of us have
had moments when we have wondered, "Why,
God?" And then we know we have a Savior who
has been there and understands our despair, and
we have His example pointing us in the right
direction. When you're in the middle of a bad
day—or worse, when you feel sure you've lost
touch with heaven and are mystified in your loneliness—aim your hard questions at God, not man.

Why? Because in life's darkest hours, there are usually no human beings with adequate answers. Counselors may analyze; associates may sympathize; experienced friends may empathize. But finite minds and feeble flesh can never satisfy us with the Presence we seek, for we truly cry for God Himself, not answers. When "bad day blues" turn black with the unanswerable, and everything you thought you knew backfires, forget human philosophies or riddling theologies. Cry out to God. He doesn't mind our complaints, and although He may seem absent, He's never far away.

—JACK HAYFORD
How to Live through a Bad Day

GOD IS ALWAYS SPEAKING

Let me state something important. There is never a time during which Jesus is not speaking. Never. There is never a place in which Jesus is not present. Never. There is never a room so dark . . . that the ever-present, ever-pursuing, relentlessly tender Friend is not there, tapping gently on the doors of our hearts—waiting to be invited in.

Few hear his voice. Fewer still open the door.

But never interpret our numbness as his absence. For amidst the fleeting promises of pleasure is the timeless promise of his presence.

"Surely I am with you always, to the very end of the age."

"Never will I leave you; never will I forsake you."

There is no chorus so loud that the voice of God cannot be heard . . . if we will but listen . . .

—MAX LUCADO
In the Eye of the Storm

❖ ❖ ❖

GOD IS FOR YOU

These questions are not new to you. You've asked them before. In the night you've asked them; in anger you've asked them. The doctor's diagnosis brought them to the surface, as did the court's decision, the phone call from the bank, and the incomprehensible tragedies that occur in our world. The questions are probes of pain and problem and circumstance. No, the questions are not new, but maybe the answers are.

If God is for us, who can be against us? (Romans 8:31 NIV)

The question is not simply "Who can be against us?" You could answer that one. Who is against you? Disease, inflation, corruption, exhaustion. Calamities confront, and fears imprison. Were the question "Who can be against us?" we could list our foes much easier than we could fight them. But that is not the question. The question is, IF GOD IS FOR US, who can be against us? . . .

God is for you. Your parents may have forgotten you, your teachers may have neglected you, your siblings may be ashamed of you, but within reach of your prayers is the maker of the oceans. God!

God *is* for you. Not "may be," not "has been," not "was," not "would be," but "God is!" He *is* for you. Today. At this hour. At this minute. As you read this sentence. No need to wait in line or come back tomorrow. He *is* with you. He could not be closer than he is at this second. His loyalty won't increase if you are better nor lessen if you are worse. He *is* for you.

God is *for* you. Turn to the sidelines; that's God cheering your run. Look past the finish line; that's God applauding your steps. Listen for him in the bleachers, shouting your name. Too tired to continue? He'll carry you. Too discouraged to fight? He's picking you up. God is *for* you.

God is for *you.* Had he a calendar, your birthday would be circled. If he drove a car, your name would be on his bumper. If there's a tree in heaven, he's carved your name in the bark. We know he has a tattoo, and we know what it says. "I have written your name on my hand," he declares (Isaiah 49:16). . . .

God is with you. Knowing that, who is against you? Can death harm you now? Can disease rob your life? Can your purpose be taken or your value diminished? No. . . .

And when bad things happen—does God care then? Does he love me in the midst of fear? Is he with me when danger lurks?

Will God stop loving me?

That's the question. That's the concern. Oh, you don't say it; you may not even know it. But I can see it on your faces. I can hear it in your words. Did I cross the line this week? Last Tuesday when I drank vodka until I couldn't walk . . . last Thursday when my business took me where I had no business being . . . last summer when I cursed the God who made me as I stood near the grave of the child he gave me?

Did I drift too far? Wait too long? Slip too much? Was I too uncertain? Too fearful? Too angry at the pain in this world?

That's what we want to know.

Can anything separate us from the love Christ has for us?

God answered our question before we asked it. So we'd see his answer, he lit the sky with a star. So we'd hear it, he filled the night with a choir; and so we'd believe it, he did what no man had ever dreamed. He became flesh and dwelt among us.

He placed his hand on the shoulder of humanity and said, "You're something special."

—MAX LUCADO
America Looks Up

Prayer and Compassion

Never Forget . . . God Listens and Loves You

✤ ✤ ✤

In the Storm, We Pray

You and I live in a loud world. To get someone's attention is no easy task. He must be willing to set everything aside to listen: turn down the radio, turn away from the monitor, turn the corner of the page and set down the book. When someone is willing to silence everything else so he can hear us clearly, it is a privilege. A rare privilege indeed.

You can talk to God because God listens. Your voice matters in heaven. He takes you very seriously. When you enter his presence, the attendants turn to you to hear your voice. No need to fear that you will be ignored. Even if you stammer or stumble, even if what you have to say impresses no one, it impresses God—and he listens. He listens to the painful plea of the elderly in the rest home. He listens to the gruff confession of the death-row inmate. When the alcoholic begs for mercy, when the spouse seeks guidance, when the businessman steps off the street into the chapel, God listens.

Intently. Carefully. The prayers are honored as

precious jewels. Purified and empowered, the words rise in a delightful fragrance to our Lord. "The smoke from the incense went up from the angel's hand to God" (Revelation 8:4). Incredible. Your words do not stop until they reach the very throne of God.

One call and heaven's fleet appears. Your prayer on earth activates God's power in heaven.

You are the someone of God's kingdom. Your prayers move God to change the world. You may not understand the mystery of prayer. You don't need to. But this much is clear: Actions in heaven begin when someone prays on earth. What an amazing thought!

When you speak, Jesus hears.

And when Jesus hears, the world is changed.

All because someone prayed.

—MAX LUCADO
America Looks Up

BECOME A COMFORTER

When we go through adversity it is so reassuring to have someone there to walk with us. It is so comforting to know our God is "the father of all comfort" who has promised never to leave us or to forsake us. One of the simple things that we can do in the midst of tragedy is to reach out to people with compassion and understanding—to walk with those in need, to comfort them. People need the loving touch, the embrace of a friend. We need someone to reach out to us in troubling times. Reaching out implies doing something, doesn't it? Compassionate people are those who feel the pain of others and *act* to alleviate that pain. . . .

The Scriptures depict God as a loving father caring for His children as a tender, nurturing nurse and as a mother hen hovering over and protecting her chicks. These metaphors are pictures of a God committed to compassionate care for His children.

A fundamental requisite for those who seek to comfort others is the ability to forget about self. It is so easy for us to become enamored of our own affairs and get caught up in our own journey to significance and success. We must work hard to put others first. Who can ever forget images of Mother Teresa in the suburbs of Calcutta pouring out her life for the poor and needy? And what about the self-sacrificing plane passengers who lost their lives while attempting to thwart the hijackers from using the plane as an instrument of further death and destruction?

We must become successful comforters by being present while others weep, by sharing a shoulder for others to lean on, and by being a reliable and careful listener. We must be dependable and trustworthy with the thoughts that are shared with us and avoid giving hasty answers or worn-out cliches to those who grieve. Grieving people need the safety of friends who hold them up rather than hold them accountable for what they express in anger and frustration. Yes, there is the great opportunity for us to be channels of mercy and comfort in the name of our Lord.

—CHARLES STANLEY
When Tragedy Strikes

❖ ❖ ❖

TO LIVE WITH COMPASSION

If someone asked you if you were compassionate, you might readily say yes. Or at least, "I believe so." But pause to examine the word *compassion* and answering gets more complicated. For the word comes from roots that mean literally to "suffer with"; to show compassion means sharing in the suffering "passion" of another. Compassion understood in this way asks more from us than a mere stirring of pity or a sympathetic word.

To live with compassion means to enter others' dark moments. It is to walk into places of pain, not to flinch or look away when another agonizes. It means to stay where people suffer. Compassion holds us back from quick, eager explanations when tragedy meets someone we know or love. . . .

In his penetrating study, *The Betrayal of the Self,* the psychoanalyst Arno Gruen shows convincingly how "the actual source of our cruelty and callousness lies in the rejection of our suffering."[1]

For we may fall into the illusion that we own people, that we can use them, that we have a right to manage their feelings. By offering premature advice on how to cope, by rushing to reassure, by prodding with advice, we say much about our own need for easy closure. When we barge in with such consolation, we make hurting souls into objects or projects. . . .

Compassion in its fullest sense can be attributed only to God. It is the central message of the gospel that God, who in no way is in competition with us, is the One who can be truly compassionate. It is because Jesus was not dependent on people, but only on God, that he could be so close to people, so concerned, so confronting, so healing, so caring. He related to people for their own sake, not his own. To say it in more psychological terms, he paid attention without intention. His question was not "How can I receive satisfaction?" but "How can I respond to your real need?" . . . Your love for others can be unconditional, without a condition that your needs are gratified, when you have the experience of being loved.

—HENRI NOUWEN
Turn My Mourning into Dancing

---

1. Arno Gruen, The Betrayal of the Self (New York: Grove, 1988), 281.

Living Fearlessly

Never Forget . . . God Knows
About Your Circumstances

❖ ❖ ❖

The Lord Is the Defense of My Life

Some of us who are old enough recall how difficult it can be to live during trying times, to face an enemy seeking to destroy all that is held sacred and dear. In such times people seek help, comfort, assurance, and safety. In moments of tragedy and crisis there is no better place to turn than to our God who has promised to help those who turn to Him in times of trouble. . . .

Many of God's saints have known times of trouble and difficulty as they journeyed through life. Consider David the psalmist of Israel. Though he was anointed and chosen to be king, he found himself hated and hunted by those who sought to destroy him. In Psalm 27, however, notice what he says while in the midst of trouble:

> The Lord is [the] light [of] my salvation;
> whom shall I fear?
> The Lord is the defense of my life;
> whom shall I dread?

When evildoers came upon me
>   to devour my flesh,
my adversaries and my enemies,
>   they stumbled and fell.
Though a host encamp against me,
>   my heart will not fear;
Though war rise against me,
>   in spite of this I shall be confident.

(VV. 1–3, NASB, emphasis added)

These are the words of a man who has learned how to be sustained in the most difficult, trying times of life. He learned an amazing lesson—in the midst of tragedy, he did not need to live in fear, because God was his defense. Though in a war zone, he could be fully confident that God would *protect* and *sustain* him.

There is hope for us because God has promised never to leave us or to forsake us. There is hope because we are not alone—we have each other. This is the strength of a nation under attack—a united spirit gaining confidence and determination from each other. But more importantly, learning to rely on our God.

—CHARLES STANLEY
When Tragedy Strikes

FACING AN UNCERTAIN FUTURE

How can we face the fog of our uneasy, uncertain future? All these terrifying events are happening—buildings collapsing, explosions all around us, anthrax and bioterrorism threats which intensify our concerns. What more can the future hold?

Verse ten of Psalm 46 answers that: ["Cease striving, and know that I am God"]. *We will not worry*. The text says, "cease striving" . . . and it means, "Stop!" What a great directive! STOP!

I heard a mother say that to one of her children in the grocery store just yesterday. The child was busy, busy, busy. Getting into this, messing with that. "Stop!" When I heard her, I *stopped!*

But it's the Lord who is speaking at this moment. "Stop! Stop it! Stop that worrying. Quit it! I am your refuge. I am your very present help in time of trouble. Your worry implies that I'm not here anymore. But I never left. I'm not like the swallows that leave in the winter, to return only when the weather is fair."

Now you see why Psalm 46 speaks with such

relevance. In times of physical catastrophe, since God is our refuge, we will not *fear*. At the threat of warfare, since God is our refuge, we will not be *moved*. With a future that seems uncertain, we will not *worry*. We'll remember He brings an end to wars. War is nothing new to Him. Chariots, spears, arrows have a way of making us churn within. But, *stop!* We will not worry. . . .

If the foundations are in place, if we have the Lord God as our refuge and strength, the righteous do not fear, are not moved, and cannot worry.

—CHARLES R. SWINDOLL
Why, God?

MY HEART WILL NOT FEAR

We are not a fearful people. We do not suddenly give up just because something frightens us. When I was about nine years of age, Pearl Harbor was attacked. The American response was unforgettable. Young men, barely sixteen or seventeen years old, lined up to enlist and to serve. They did not care which branch of service would take them; they only wanted to defend their nation.

When united, this country trembles before no other power. We have a national sense of courage and bravery. We have a heritage of firmness and determination that has carried us through many troubling and dangerous times. I want to remind you of this so that none of us will expect anything less from our nation than a determined, courageous response to the task ahead. Doris Dougherty captured this moment accurately when she said, "No greater tragedy can be found than that of a soul crying out 'It's not fair!' and allowing the cold waters of cynicism to overflow and to drown him." She continues that there is no greater victory than to plunge into these waters where the bottom cannot be felt, but the strong person will "swim until I can!" We may not be able to feel the bottom right now, but our country will swim until we do!

In the 1940s America began fighting a war in the Pacific and soon thereafter a war in Europe as well. Back then, America was not heavily industrialized; we were mostly a nation of farmers. We were unprepared for war, and yet we successfully fought on two fronts for four long years. The cost was devastatingly high, but we were triumphant, which says something about our bravery, determination, and national character. . . .

We have a right to be a godly people who are fearless. We have a right to be bold and confident for the simple reason that God has promised to intervene in our behalf. Does that mean that we will never suffer consequences? No, it does not. Will we always be free from hardship and adversity? Of course not. It means that when we, as individuals or as a nation, stand sovereign under the protection of God, then we can be assured that He will not fail us. No matter neither the disaster that we face nor the enemy at our gate, with our God we will be triumphant.

We can never know what transpired in the hearts and minds of those men and women who died in the collapse of the World Trade Center buildings, but I am sure that many, knowing that they were about to die, courageously committed themselves into the arms of a loving God. One whose arms were there to shield them from the steel and rubble and usher them gently to their heavenly reward.

There is an old gospel song by Charles Tindley that states, "We'll understand it better by and by." Only in eternity will we understand some of the mysterious ways of almighty God. Only then will we grasp the significance of His eternal plan that encompasses all of us.

—CHARLES STANLEY
When Tragedy Strikes

Hope

*Never Forget . . . God Gives
You Promises for a Future*

❖ ❖ ❖

Looking Forward

Death is the great equalizer, isn't it? It doesn't matter if we have lived on this earth as:

    young or old
        rich or poor
            famous or unknown
                educated or ignorant
                  powerful or weak
                    religious or atheistic
                      athletic or crippled
                    healthy or sickly
                        happy or depressed . . .
                        we all die.[1]

Still, death can come as an utterly unexpected surprise. More than five thousand men and women went to work at the World Trade Center in New York City on September 11, 2001, and began what they thought was just another routine day at the office. Many of them had likely gotten a cup of coffee, sat down at their desks, rolled up their sleeves, booted up their computers, and begun placing telephone calls. None of them had any indication that within the hour they would step into eternity. For them, death came as a thief in the night.

For others, death can come as a longed-for and welcomed relief. Within a three-week period, while I was in the midst of writing this book, I attended both the funeral of my husband's beloved brother, John Lotz, and the funeral of my father's associate T. W. Wilson, who was like a second father to me. John died as a result of a fast-growing, malignant brain tumor. "Uncle T" died from massive heart failure at the grand old age of eighty-two. For both John and Uncle T, death came as an angel of mercy.

Regardless of how or when it comes, death does come for each of us. And each of us wonders: *When will it come for my loved one? What will it be like for me?*

For the past thirteen years I have traveled all over the world in response to invitations to give out God's Word. There have been times, such as my first visit to India, when I have started out by climbing onto the plane with my stomach churning, my knees knocking, and my heart fibrillating—terrified because I was not sure where I was going, or who would meet me at the journey's end. But what a difference there has been in my attitude when I have had the opportunity for a second visit to that same place. I have left home with peace in my heart because I knew where I was going and who would meet me at the journey's end. In the same way, the prospect of death can fill you and me with terror and dread—unless we know where we are going. Knowing as much as we can about our final destination, and Who will meet us at the end of life's journey, takes the fear out of getting there. . . .

Are you facing the future with eyes wide shut, teeth clenched, body tensed, dreading your tomorrows and what they may hold? Do you feel as though you are standing on the brink of a deep, dark abyss of helplessness and despair, caught up in events involving yourself or your loved ones that are beyond your control? Regardless of what those events may be, no matter your mental or emotional or spiritual state, God's vision of the future can fill you with hope right now. . . .

As I contemplate the deaths of my loved ones— and yours . . .

As I contemplate our loss and the empty void in our hearts left by their absence . . .

I am more grateful than ever that this life is not all there is!

Praise God! You and I can look *forward WITH HOPE!* because we have the blessed assurance of Heaven, My Father's House!

—ANNE GRAHAM LOTZ
Heaven: My Father's House

---

1. See Hebrews 9:27.

❖ ❖ ❖

HOPE RESTORED

For many people, life is—well, life is a jungle. Not a jungle of trees and beasts. Would that it were so simple. Would that our jungles could be cut with a machete or our adversaries trapped in a cage. But our jungles are comprised of the thicker thickets of failing health, broken hearts, and empty wallets. Our forests are framed with hospital walls and divorce courts. We don't hear the screeching of birds or the roaring of lions, but we do hear the complaints of neighbors and the demands of bosses. Our predators are our creditors, and the brush that surrounds us is the rush that exhausts us.

It's a jungle out there.

And for some, even many, hope is in short supply. . . .

What would it take to restore your hope? . . .

Our Shepherd majors in restoring hope to the soul. Whether you are a lamb lost on a craggy ledge or a city slicker alone in a deep jungle, everything changes when your rescuer appears.

Your loneliness diminishes, because you have fellowship.

Your despair decreases, because you have vision.

Your confusion begins to lift, because you have direction.

Please note: You have left the jungle. The trees still eclipse the sky, and the thorns still cut the skin. Animals lurk and rodents scurry. The jungle is still a jungle. It hasn't changed, but you have. You have changed because you have hope. And you have hope because you have met someone who can lead you out.

Your Shepherd knows that you were not made for this place. He knows you are not equipped for this place. So he has come to guide you out.

He has come to restore your soul.

Jesus doesn't give hope by changing the jungle; he restores our hope by giving us himself. And he has promised to stay until the very end: "I am with you always to the very end of the age." (Matthew 28:20 NIV).

—MAX LUCADO
Traveling Light

❖ ❖ ❖

THE FORWARD LOOK

We will experience the minutes and hours and days of our lives differently when hope takes up residence. In a letter to Jim Forest, who at the time directed the Fellowship of Reconciliation, Thomas Merton wrote, "The real hope is not in something we think we can do, but in God, who is making something good out of it in some way we cannot see."

Hope is not dependent on peace in the land, justice in the world, and success in the business. Hope is willing to leave unanswered questions unanswered and unknown futures unknown. Hope makes you see God's guiding hand not only in the gentle and pleasant moments but also in the shadows of disappointment and darkness.

No one can truly say with certainty where he

or she will be ten or twenty years from now. You do not know if you will be free or in captivity, if you will be honored or despised, if you will have many friends or few, if you will be liked or rejected. But when you hold lightly these dreams and fears, you can be open to receive every day as a new day and to live your life as a unique expression of God's love for humankind. . . .

A soldier was captured as a prisoner of war. His captors transported him by train far from his homeland. He felt isolated from country, bereft of family, estranged from anything familiar. His loneliness grew as he continued not to hear anything from home. He could not know that his family was even alive, how his country was faring. He had lost a sense of anything to live for.

But suddenly, unexpectedly, he got a letter. It was smudged, torn at the edges from months of travel. But it said, "We are waiting for you to come home. All is fine here. Don't worry." Everything instantly seemed different. His circumstances had not changed. He did the same difficult labor on the same meager rations, but now he knew someone waited for his release and homecoming. Hope changed his life.

God has written us a letter. The good news of

God's revelation in Christ declares to us precisely what we need to hope. Sometimes the words of the Bible do not seem important to us. Or they do not appeal to us. But in those words we hear Christ saying in effect, "I am waiting for you. I am preparing a house for you and there are many rooms in my house." Paul the Apostle tells us, "Be transformed by the renewing of your minds" (Romans 12:2 NSRV). We hear a promise and an invitation to a life we could not dream of if all we considered were our own resources.

Therein is the hope that gives us new power to live, new strength. We find a way, even in sadness and illness and even death, never to forget how we can hope.

We catch glimmers of this way to live even while we must admit how dimly we see it and imperfectly we live it. "I am holding on to my conviction that I can trust God," I must tell myself sometimes, "since I cannot yet say it fully." I dare to say it even when everything is not perfect, when I know others will criticize my actions, when I fear that my limitations will disappoint many—and myself. But still I trust that the truth will shine through, even when I cannot fully grasp it. Still I believe that God will accomplish what I cannot, in God's own grace and unfathomable might.

The paradox of expectation is that those who believe in tomorrow can better live today; those who expect joy to come out of sadness can discover the beginnings of a new life amid the old; those who look forward to the returning Lord can discover him already in their midst. Just as the love of a mother for her son can grow while she is waiting for his return, just as lovers can rediscover each other after long periods of absence, so our intimate relationship with God can become deeper and more mature while we wait patiently in expectation of his return.

To hope for this growth, to believe even in its possibility, is to say no to every form of fatalism. It is to voice a no to every way we tell ourselves "I know myself—I cannot expect any changes." This no to discouragement and self-despair comes in the context of a yes to life, a yes we say amid even fragile times lived in a world of impatience and violence. For even while we mourn, we do not forget how our life can ultimately join God's larger dance of life and hope.

—HENRI NOUWEN
Turn My Mourning into Dancing

✣ ✣ ✣

A Home That Is Safe

On September 11, 2001, like millions of other Americans, I sat glued to my television set. The horrifying scenes of the jetliners crashing into the towers and the Pentagon, the erupting fireballs, and the imploding buildings that were played over and over again are indelibly frozen in my mind's eye.

I wonder how many parents were faced with teary, terrified children who returned home from school that Tuesday afternoon asking, "Mommy, Daddy, are we at war? Are we going to die? Will we be safe?" How did the parents answer? Did they speak the truth? Or did they just give hollow words of comfort because they had no answers?

While we cannot guarantee the safety of our children, or ourselves, or anyone else in this life, Jesus Christ does guarantee our safety in eternity. When you and I place our faith in Him as our Savior and yield our lives to Him as Lord, God promises that we "shall not perish but have eternal life" (John 3:16 NIV). And the "eternal life" will be lived with God and His family in My Father's House! . . .

Heaven is a very real place that will give you very real freedom. You need never fear. . . .

> hijackers or bombers, terrorists or threats,
> lawsuits or gunshots, bullets or bandits,
> boundaries that stifle, roadblocks that stop,
> limits that squelch, walls that strangle,
> planes that crash, buildings that implode . . .

The Creator Who created all the earthly beauty we have grown to love . . .

> The majestic snowcapped peaks of
> the Alps,
> The rushing mountain streams,
> The brilliantly colored fall leaves,
> The carpets of wildflowers,
> The glistening fin of a fish as it leaps out
> of a sparkling sea,
> The graceful gliding of a swan across
> the lake,
> The lilting notes of a canary's song,
> The whir of a hummingbird's wings,
> The shimmer of the dew on the grass
> in early morning . . .

If God could make the heavens and earth as beautiful as we think they are today—which includes thousands of years of wear and tear, corruption and pollution, sin and selfishness—can you imagine what the new Heaven and the new earth will look like? It will be much more glorious than any eyes have seen, any ears have heard, or any minds have ever conceived![1]

—ANNE GRAHAM LOTZ
Heaven: My Father's House

---

1. See 1 Corinthians 2:9.

An Invitation

Never Forget . . . God Longs
for You to Know Him

❖ ❖ ❖

He Did This Just for You

For God so loved the world that he gave his one and only Son, that whoever believes in him shall not perish but have eternal life.

John 3:16 (NIV)

Note what God did: ". . . He gave his only Son." This is how he dealt with your sin. Imagine it this way. Suppose you are found guilty of a crime. You are in a courtroom in front of the judge, and he sentences you to death for your crime. His sentence is just. You are guilty, and the punishment for your crime is death. But suppose that the judge is your father. He knows the law; he knows that your crime demands a death. But he knows love; he knows that he loves you too much to let you die. So in a wonderful act of love, he stands and removes his robe and stands by your side and says, "I'm going to die in your place."

That is what God did for you. The wages of sin is death. Heaven's justice demands a death for your sin. Heaven's love, however, can't bear to see you die. So here is what God did. He stood and removed his heavenly robes. He came to earth to tell us he would die for us. He would be our Savior. And that is what he did.

"God put the world square with himself through the Messiah, giving the world a fresh start by offering forgiveness of sins . . . God put on him the wrong who never did anything wrong, so we could be put right with God" (2 Corinthians 5:19, 21, MSG).

What does God want you to do? He wants you to get on his bus. How is this done? Three simple steps: admit, agree, accept.

1. **Admit** that God has not been first place in your life, and ask him to forgive your sins.

"If we confess our sins to him, he is faithful and just to forgive us and to cleanse us from every wrong" (1 John 1:9 NLT).

2. **Agree** that Jesus died to pay for your sins and that he rose from the dead and is alive today.

"If you confess with your mouth, 'Jesus is Lord,' and believe in your heart that God raised him from the dead, you will be saved" (Romans 10:9, NIV).

"Salvation is found in no one else [Jesus], for

there is no other name by which we must be saved" (Acts 4:12, NIV).

3. Accept God's free gift of salvation. Don't try to earn it.

"For it is by grace you have been saved, through faith—and this is not from yourselves, it is the gift of God—not by works, so that no one can boast" (Ephesians 2:8, 9 NIV).

"To all who received him, he gave the right to become children of God. All they needed to do was to trust him to save them. All those who believe this are reborn!—not a physical rebirth . . . but from the will of God" (John 1:12 ,13, TLB).

Jesus says, "Here I am! I stand at the door and knock. If anyone hears my voice and opens the door, I will come in . . ." (Revelation 3:20, NIV).

With all of my heart, I urge you to accept God's destiny for your life. I urge you to get on board with Christ. According to the Bible, "Jesus is the only One who can save people. His name is the only power in the world that has been given to save people. We must be saved through him" (Acts 4:12).

Would you let him save you? This is the most important decision you will ever make. Why don't you give your heart to him right now? **Admit** your need. **Agree** with his work. **Accept** his gift. Go to God in prayer and tell him, *I am a sinner in need of grace. I believe that Jesus died for me on the cross. I accept your offer of salvation.* It's a simple prayer with eternal results.

I believe that Jesus Christ is the Son of the Living God. I want him to be the Lord of my life.

Signed _____

Date _____

Acknowledgments

JACK HAYFORD, excerpted by permission of Thomas Nelson Publishers from the book entitled *How to Live Through a Bad Day,* copyright date 2001 by Jack Hayford.

ANNE GRAHAM LOTZ, *Heaven: My Father's House,* 2001, W Publishing Group, Nashville, Tennessee. All rights reserved.

MAX LUCADO, *America Looks Up,* 2001, W Publishing Group, Nashville, Tennessee. All rights reserved.
—*He Did This Just for You,* 2000, W Publishing Group, Nashville, Tennessee. All rights reserved.
—*In the Eye of the Storm,* 1991, W Publishing Group, Nashville, Tennessee. All rights reserved.
—*Traveling Light,* 2001, W Publishing Group, Nashville, Tennessee. All rights reserved.

HENRI NOUWEN LITERARY CENTRE, *Turn My Mourning into Dancing,* 2001, W Publishing Group, Nashville, Tennessee. All rights reserved.

ACKNOWLEDGMENTS

CHARLES STANLEY, excerpted by permission of Thomas Nelson Publishers from the book entitled *When Tragedy Strikes,* copyright date 2001 by Charles F. Stanley.

CHARLES SWINDOLL, *Why, God?,* 2001, W Publishing Group, Nashville, Tennessee. All rights reserved.